JUS

5

INGREDIENTS

LOW CALORIE

An Hachette UK Company
www.hachette.co.uk

First published in Great Britain in 2015 by
Hamlyn, a division of Octopus Publishing Group Ltd
Endeavour House
189 Shaftesbury Avenue
London
WC2H 8JY
www.octopusbooks.co.uk
www.octopusbooksusa.com

Distributed in the US by Hachette Book Group
1290 Avenue of the Americas, 4th and 5th Floors
New York, NY 10020

Distributed in Canada by Canadian Manda Group
664 Annette St, Toronto, Ontario, Canada M6S 2C8

Some of the recipes in this book have previously been published by Hamlyn.

ISBN 978-0-60062-841-5

A CIP catalogue record for this book is available from the British Library

Printed and bound in China

10 9 8 7 6 5 4 3 2 1

Commissioning Editor Eleanor Maxfield
Editor Pauline Bache
Designers Jeremy Tilston, Jaz Bahra & Eoghan O'Brien
Assistant Production Manager Caroline Alberti

Standard level spoon and cup measurements are used in all recipes.

Eggs should be large unless otherwise stated. The U.S. Food and Drug
Administration advises that eggs should not be consumed raw. This book contains
dishes made with raw or lightly cooked eggs. It is prudent for more vulnerable
people, such as pregnant and nursing mothers, people with a weakened immune
system, the elderly, babies, and young children, to avoid uncooked or lightly cooked
dishes made with eggs. Once prepared, these dishes should be kept refrigerated and
used promptly.

Milk should be whole unless otherwise stated.

Ovens should be preheated to the specific temperature; if using a convection oven,
follow manufacturer's instructions for adjusting the time and the temperature.

All microwave information is based on a 650 watt oven. Follow manufacturer's
instructions for an oven with a different wattage.

This book includes dishes made with nuts and nut derivatives. It is advisable for
customers with known allergic reactions to nuts and nut derivatives and those
who may be potentially vulnerable to these allergies, such as pregnant and nursing
mothers, people with a weakend immune system, the elderly, babies, and children,
to avoid dishes made with nuts and nut oils. It is also prudent to check the labels of
prepared Ingredients for the possible inclusion of nut derivatives.

JUST 5 INGREDIENTS

LOW CALORIE

MAKE LIFE SIMPLE WITH MORE THAN 100 RECIPES USING 5 INGREDIENTS OR FEWER

hamlyn

CONTENTS

INTRODUCTION

The recipes in this book have been chosen not only for their simplicity and great flavors, but also because they use just five or fewer main ingredients.

Applying a five-ingredient approach to cooking will help you create a repertoire of quick, easy, adaptable dishes, that are not only cheap and tasty but that also require little shopping and preparation. You will learn to master some basic recipes in record time and come to appreciate that cooking for yourself is a satisfying and empowering process.

This will make your life easier in three ways. First, because the recipes are straightforward there is less fussy preparation, which will save you time. Second, you will find that shopping is simpler. How long do you really want to wander around a supermarket searching for something to cook? And third, it will save money. The five-ingredient approach will mean that you don't have a fridge full of half-used packages of strange ingredients left over from previous meals.

Unlike other five-ingredient cookbooks, you won't have hundreds of hidden added extras to stock up on. This series requires you to remember ten pantry extras only—simple, easy-to-remember basics you will no doubt already have at hand.

Start by stocking up on your pantry ten (see page 11). Make sure you have at least some of them at all times so that you are just five ingredients away from a decent meal.

Next, choose a recipe that suits the time you have to cook, your energy levels, and your mood. Check what pantry ingredients you will need on the list. The five key ingredients you will need to complete the dish are clearly numbered.

One of the best ways to eat cheaply is to avoid costly processed foods. Instead, buy basic ingredients such as vegetables, rice, pasta, fish, and chicken, and build your meals around these. You should also try to avoid waste and not spend money on food you don't eat and that has to be thrown away. Buy food that lasts and plan around the lifetime dates of foods. If you have a freezer, freeze the leftovers for another day.

Plan your meals for the week so you need to go shopping only once a week. When you get into the habit of doing this the ingredients for each meal will be waiting when you need them. Buy in bulk to get the best prices. Make time to shop around and compare prices in the nearest supermarket, online, your local stores and at market stalls to see which is cheapest. Stick to buying fruit and vegetables that are in season.

Not only will they be better value than exotic produce flown in from abroad but you will be reducing your food miles. Finally, don't even think about spending precious cash on a supermarket's special offer unless it is something you will actually use. Three tins of sardines in mustard sauce for the price of one is a good value only if you are going to eat them.

This book offers a range of delicious recipes that are low in calories but still high in flavor. Each recipe shows a calorie count per portion, so you will know exactly what you are eating. These are recipes for real and delicious food, not ultra-slimming meals, so they will help you maintain a healthier eating plan for life. They must be used as part of a balanced diet, with the cakes and sweet dishes eaten only as an occasional treat.

As we all know, one of the major causes of obesity is eating too many calories. Based on our relatively inactive modern-day lifestyles, most nutritionists recommend that women should aim to consume around 2,000 calories (kcal) per day, and men an amount of around 2,500. For a woman, the aim is to reduce her daily calorie intake to around 1,500 kcal while she is trying to lose weight, then settle on around 2,000 per day thereafter to maintain her new body weight. As a general guide, adults should aim to undertake at least 30 minutes of moderate-intensity exercise, such as a brisk walk, five times a week. The 30 minutes does not have to be done at once: three sessions of 10 minutes are equally beneficial. Children and young people should be encouraged to do at least 60 minutes of moderate-intensity exercise every day.

Remember

Eat more fruit and vegetables, aiming for at least five portions of different fruit and vegetables a day (excluding potatoes). Eat fewer sugary foods and look out for hidden sugar. This will also help reduce your fat intake. Low-fat versions are available for most dairy products, including milk, cheese, sour cream, yogurt, and even cream and butter. Choose lean cuts of meat, and chicken breasts instead of thighs. Trim all visible fat off meat before cooking and avoid frying foods—grill or roast instead. Fish is naturally low in fat and can make tempting dishes.

Above all, enjoy trying out the new flavors and exciting recipes that this book contains. Rather than dwelling on the thought that you are denying yourself your usual unhealthy treats, think of your new regime as a positive step towards a new you.

Enjoy!

WEEKLY PLANNER

SUPERFOODS

MONDAY
Walnut & Banana Sunrise Smoothie (see page 34)

TUESDAY
Warm Eggplant Salad (see page 38)

WEDNESDAY
Coconut Citrus Squid (see page 152)

THURSDAY
Spinach & Ricotta Frittata (see page 114)

FRIDAY
Moroccan Grilled Sardines (see page 144)

SATURDAY
Lemon Grass Chicken (see page 116)

PANTRY 10

The only extras you will need!

1 Sugars
2 Flours
3 Oils & vinegars
4 Baking Powder
5 Salt
6 Pepper
7 Stock
8 Onion
9 Garlic
10 Lemon & lemon juice

SHOPPING LIST

- 10–12 prepared baby squid, about 12 oz including tentacles
- 12 sardines
- 12 large chicken drumsticks
- 4 trout fillets, about 7 oz each
- 2 tablespoons capers
- 1 (13 oz) can butter beans
- 2 tablespoons harissa
- 2 tablespoons medium curry paste
- 1 orange
- 1 banana
- 1 oz walnut pieces
- 2 eggplants
- 4 tomatoes
- 6 limes
- 3 red chiles
- 1 inch piece of fresh root ginger
- 3½ oz freshly grated coconut
- 7 oz baby spinach leaves
- 6 tablespoons very finely chopped lemon grass
- 1 lemon grass stalk
- lettuce or other greens
- 4 tablespoons chopped parsley
- chopped cilantro
- large handful of basil
- ¼ pint skimmed milk
- 5 oz natural yogurt
- 4 eggs
- 2 oz ricotta cheese
- 2 oz Parmesan cheese

SUNDAY
Trout with Pesto (see page 110)

WEEKLY PLANNER

DETOX

MONDAY
Tuna & Borlotti Bean Salad (see page 56)

TUESDAY
Chicken & Vegetable Skewers (see page 76)

WEDNESDAY
Sweet Potato & Cabbage Soup (see page 84)

THURSDAY
Langoustines with Tamarind & Lime (see page 86)

FRIDAY
Grilled Tuna Salad (see page 106)

SATURDAY
Chile & Cilantro Fish Parcels (see page 128)

PANTRY 10

The only extras you will need!

1 Sugars
2 Flours
3 Oils & vinegars
4 Baking Powder
5 Salt
6 Pepper
7 Stock
8 Onion
9 Garlic
10 Lemon & lemon juice

SHOPPING LIST

- 4 chicken thighs
- 4 lean bacon
- 2 lb large, uncooked langoustines in their shell
- 1 lb boneless, skinless chicken breasts
- 4 oz cod or haddock fillet
- 4 fresh tuna steaks, about 6 oz each
- 1 (13 oz) can borlotti beans
- 1 (7 oz) can tuna in olive oil
- 2 tablespoons honey
- 2 tablespoons mild wholegrain mustard
- 2 teaspoons tamarind paste
- 1 red chile
- 2 celery sticks
- 2 oz arugula
- 3½ oz baby spinach leaves, roughly chopped
- 1 zucchini
- 1 carrot
- 1 lb sweet potatoes
- 1 lb small new potatoes
- 2 parsnips
- 1 baby Savoy cabbage
- 1½ inch piece of fresh ginger
- 4 limes
- 1 green chile
- 1 scallion
- 1 teaspoon chopped thyme
- medium bunch of cilantro
- 2 teaspoons natural yogurt
- 1 egg

SUNDAY
Low-fat Lemon Chicken (see page 148)

5 FOR VEGETARIANS

With only 5 key ingredients, these veggie meals with satisfy vegetarians and meat eaters alike. Helping you toward your recommended 5-a-day, they are packed with vitamins and nutrients, too.

Moroccan Chickpea Salad (see page 46)

Wild Mushroom Omelette (see page 70)

Vegetable Curry (see page 64)

Pepper & Walnut Papparadelle (see page 118)

Butternut Squash & Ricotta Frittata (see page 72)

5 FOR CHICKEN

Lean, quick, and easily available, chicken is the perfect meat to eat when watching your weight, and it's a great base for absorbing all the flavors from your 5 ingredients.

Grilled Summer Chicken Salad (see page 98)   Seared Chicken Sandwich (see page 44)

Greek Chicken Avgolomeno (see page 82)   Fast Chicken Curry (see page 108)

Chicken with Orange & Mint (see page 142)

5 FOR FISH & SEAFOOD

While fish is a great, tasty source of protein, some people are intimidated at the prospect of preparing fish dishes, but with just 5 key ingredients, these dishes are so simple you'll be gaining confidence and eating in no time!

Baked Cod with Tomatoes & Olives (see page 60)

Bass with Tomato & Basil Sauce (see page 68)

Smoked Salmon Risotto (see page 120)

Swordfish with Couscous & Salsa (see page 132)

Warm Scallop Salad (see page 48)

5 FOR SUMMER SUPPERS

Summer is the time when the pressure's on to be in your best shape ever, and these light, refreshing suppers are perfect to choose for al fresco eating, and making the most of the long days.

Bean, Polish Sausage & Pepper Salad (see page 50)

Prosciutto & Arugula Pizza (see page 92)

Watermelon & Feta Salad (see page 52)

Chicken Teriyaki (see page 94)

Grilled Bananas with Blueberries (see page 182)

5 FOR WARMING UP

Healthy, low-calorie food doesn't mean you have to compromise at those times when comfort food is what's needed, and these warming, indulgent dishes provide winter treats, without any of the usual naughtiness.

Pumpkin & Goat Cheese Casserole (see page 66)

Bacon & White Bean Soup (see page 74)

Pepper-crusted Loin of Venison (see page 130)

Poached Peaches & Raspberries (see page 88)

Calves' Liver with Mashed Potato (see page 100)

5 FOR EASTERN FLAVOR

Thai, Indian, Chinese, and Japanese food all pack in the flavor without soaring calories and, with only 5 ingredients each in these recipes, you won't have to spend hours traipsing the supermarket aisles to take your tastebuds on a journey.

Chai Teabread (see page 24)

Thai Red Pork & Bean Curry (see page 80)

Sugar & Spice Salmon (see page 138)

Lychee & Coconut Sherbet (see page 186)

Grilled Tandoori Chicken (see page 112)

SNACKS, SALADS, & LIGHT BITES

MAKES 2 × ½ PINT GLASSES

Calories per serving 89
Preparation time 2 minutes

INGREDIENTS

1	1 ripe peach, halved, pitted, and chopped
2	5 oz strawberries
3	5 oz raspberries
4	7 fl oz milk
5	ice cubes

Fruity Summer Milkshakes

■ Put the peach in a blender or food processor with the strawberries and raspberries and blend to a smooth purée, scraping the mixture down from the sides of the bowl if necessary.

■ Add the milk and blend the ingredients again until the mixture is smooth and frothy. Pour the milkshake over the ice cubes in tall glasses.

Calories per serving 302
Preparation time 15 minutes, plus standing
Cooking time 1¼ hours

INGREDIENTS

| **1** | **5 chai tea bags** |

| **2** | **10 oz mixed dried fruit** |

| **3** | **2 oz Brazil nuts, chopped** |

| **4** | **3½ tablespoons butter** |

| **5** | **1 egg, beaten** |

PANTRY

½ pint boiling water; 2 cups all-purpose flour; 1 teaspoon baking powder; ¾ cup firmly packed light brown sugar

Chai Teabread

■ Stir the tea bags into the water and let stand for 10 minutes.

■ Mix together the flour, baking powder, sugar, dried fruit, and nuts in a bowl. Remove the tea bags from the water, squeezing out all the water. Thinly slice the butter into the tea and stir until melted. Let cool slightly. Add to the dry ingredients with the egg and mix together well.

■ Spoon the mixture into a greased and lined 2 lb or 2¼ pint loaf tin and spread the mixture right into the corners. Bake in a preheated oven, at 325°F, for 1¼ hours or until risen, firm and a toothpick inserted into the center comes out clean. Loosen the cake and transfer to a wire rack. Peel off the lining paper and let cool. Spread the top with Chai Cream Frosting, if desired (see right).

FOR CHAI CREAM FROSTING

Put 2 fl oz milk and 3 chai tea bags in a saucepan and bring to a boil. Remove from the heat and leave until cold. Discard the tea bags, squeezing them to extract the liquid. Beat together 7 oz cream cheese and 2 tablespoons very soft unsalted butter in a bowl until smooth. Beat in the flavored milk and ¾ cup sifted confectioners' sugar. Calories per serving 113

Calories per muffin 172
Preparation time 10 minutes
Cooking time 20 minutes

INGREDIENTS

1   **3 pieces candied ginger from a jar, about 2 oz, finely chopped**

2   **3½ oz dried cranberries**

3   **1 egg**

4   **8 fl oz milk**

PANTRY

2½ cups all-purpose flour; 1 tablespoon baking powder; ⅓ cup firmly packed light brown sugar; ¼ cup vegetable oil

Cranberry Muffins

■ Line a 12-section muffin pan with paper muffin cases. Sift the flour and baking powder into a large bowl. Stir in the sugar, ginger, and cranberries until evenly distributed.

■ Beat together the egg, milk, and oil in a separate bowl, then add the liquid to the flour mixture. Using a large metal spoon, gently stir the liquid into the flour, until only just combined. The mixture should look craggy, with specks of flour still visible.

■ Divide the mixture between the muffin cases, piling it up in the center. Bake in a preheated oven, at 400°F, for 18–20 minutes, until well risen and golden. Transfer to a wire rack and serve while still slightly warm.

Calories per serving 348
Preparation time 5 minutes, plus chilling

INGREDIENTS

1	2 passion fruit
2	8 fl oz natural yogurt
3	¼ cup honey
4	2 oz hazelnuts, toasted and roughly chopped
5	4 clementines, peeled and chopped into small pieces

Nutty Passion Fruit Yogurts

■ Halve the passion fruit and scoop the pulp into a large bowl. Add the yogurt and mix them together gently.

■ Put 2 tablespoons of the honey in the bases of two narrow glasses and sprinkle with half of the hazelnuts. Spoon half of the yogurt over the nuts and arrange half of the clementine pieces on top of the yogurt.

■ Repeat the layering, reserving a few of the nuts for decoration. Sprinkle the nuts over the top and chill the yogurts until you are ready to serve them.

MAKES 12

Calories per serving 120
Preparation time 20 minutes
Cooking time about 10 minutes

INGREDIENTS

1	3½ tablespoons butter, diced
2	2 oz golden raisins
3	grated zest of 1 orange
4	1 egg
5	about 4 fl oz milk

PANTRY

1 cup all-purpose flour, plus extra for dusting; ¾ cup wholewheat flour; 2 teaspoons baking powder; 1 tablespoon superfine sugar

Orange & Golden Raisin Scones

■ Sift the flours and baking powder into a large bowl, adding any bran in the sieve back into the bowl. Add the butter and rub in with the fingertips until the mixture resembles fine bread crumbs, then stir in the golden raisins, sugar, and orange zest.

■ Break the egg into a measuring cup and beat with a fork. Cover with milk up to ¼ pint, pour into the flour mixture and form a soft dough, adding a little extra milk if the dough is too dry.

■ Press gently into a circle ½ inch thick, and stamp out about 12 scones. Place them on lightly floured baking sheets and brush with a little milk. Bake in a preheated oven, at 425°F, for about 10 minutes or until risen and golden. Allow the scones to cool on a wire rack. The scones can be stored in an airtight container for up to 3 days.

MAKES 12

Calories per muffin 214
Preparation time 15 minutes
Cooking time 25 minutes

INGREDIENTS

| 1 | 1 egg, beaten |

| 2 | 7 fl oz milk |

| 3 | 7 oz mixed berries, chopped |

PANTRY

2 cups all-purpose flour; 4 tablespoons superfine sugar; 1 tablespoon baking powder; 2 fl oz vegetable oil

Very Berry Muffins

■ Mix together all of the ingredients, except the berries, to make a smooth dough. Fold in the berries.

■ Put nonstick paper cases in a 12-section muffin pan and spoon the mixture into the cases. Bake in a preheated oven, at 350°F, for 25 minutes or until a toothpick comes out clean when inserted. Transfer to a wire rack to cool.

SERVES 2

Calories per serving 265
Preparation time 5 minutes

INGREDIENTS

1	1 orange, segmented
2	1 banana
3	¼ pint skim milk
4	5 oz natural yogurt
5	1 oz walnut pieces

Walnut & Banana Sunrise Smoothie

■ Place all the ingredients in a food processor or blender and process until the mixture is smooth and frothy. Pour into 2 glasses and serve.

SERVES 4

Calories per serving 171
Preparation time 5 minutes
Cooking time 5 minutes

INGREDIENTS

1	8 large blinis
2	2 tablespoons light sour cream
3	1 teaspoon chopped dill
4	2 scallions, sliced
5	3½ oz smoked salmon

PANTRY

grated zest of 1 lemon; lemon wedges, to garnish; black pepper

Smoked Salmon Blinis with Dill Cream

■ Gently warm the blinis for a few minutes under a broiler or in the oven.

■ Stir together the sour cream, dill, lemon zest, and scallions and season with pepper. Spoon the mixture onto the blinis and top with the salmon. Garnish with lemon wedges and serve.

SERVES 4

Calories per serving 99
Preparation time 10 minutes, plus cooling
Cooking time 10 minutes

INGREDIENTS

1	2 eggplants, cut into small cubes
2	2 tablespoons capers, coarsely chopped
3	4 tomatoes, diced
4	4¼ cups chopped parsley

PANTRY

2 tablespoons olive oil; 1 red onion, finely sliced;
1 tablespoon balsamic vinegar

Warm Eggplant Salad

■ Heat the oil in a nonstick skillet. Add
the eggplant and sauté for 10 minutes until
golden and softened. Add the red onion,
capers, tomatoes, parsley, and vinegar and
stir to combine.

■ Remove the pan from the heat and let
cool for 10 minutes before serving.

SERVES 4

Calories per serving 278
Preparation time 20 minutes
Cooking time 30 minutes

INGREDIENTS

1 4 shallots, thinly sliced

2 8 eggs, lightly beaten

3 2 tablespoons finely chopped fresh mixed herbs, such as chives, chervil, parsley, basil, and thyme

4 7 oz yellow and red cherry tomatoes, halved

5 5 oz wafer-thin smoked ham slices

PANTRY

¼ cup extra virgin rapeseed oil; salt and black pepper

Ham & Tomato Omelets

■ Heat 1 teaspoon of the oil in a medium-sized skillet over medium-low heat, add the shallots and cook gently for 4–5 minutes or until softened.

■ Meanwhile, beat together the eggs and herbs in a large bowl and season with salt and pepper.

■ Remove three-quarters of the shallots from the pan with a slotted spoon and set aside. Pour one-quarter of the egg mixture into the pan, then sprinkle over one-quarter of the cherry tomatoes and stir gently, using a heat-resistant rubber spatula, until the egg is almost set. Sprinkle one-quarter of the sliced ham evenly over the top of the omelet and cook gently for another minute.

■ Fold the omelet in half, slide out of the pan onto a warm plate and serve immediately. Repeat with the remaining ingredients to make 3 more omelets. Alternatively, keep the cooked omelets warm until all 4 are ready and serve at the same time.

SERVES 4

Calories per serving 262
Preparation time 10 minutes
Cooking time 5 minutes

INGREDIENTS

1 4 scallions, sliced

2 2 (13 oz) cans green lentils, drained and rinsed

3 3 tablespoons chopped herbs (such as parsley, oregano, or basil)

4 4 oz cherry tomatoes, halved

5 3¼ oz sliced prosciutto

PANTRY

2 tablespoons olive oil; 1 garlic clove, crushed; 2 tablespoons balsamic vinegar

Herbed Lentil Salad with Prosciutto Crisps

■ Heat the oil in a nonstick saucepan, add the garlic and scallions and sauté together for 2 minutes.

■ Stir in the lentils, vinegar, herbs and tomatoes and set aside.

■ Heat a skillet until hot, add the prosciutto and cook for 1–2 minutes, until crisp. Arrange the lentil salad on a large serving dish, place the ham on top and serve immediately.

SERVES 4

Calories per serving 293
Preparation time 15 minutes
Cooking time 5–6 minutes

INGREDIENTS

1   8 oz mini chicken breasts

2   8 slices multigrain bread

3   6 tablespoons low-fat natural yogurt

4   ½–1 teaspoon freshly grated hot horseradish or horseradish sauce, to taste

5   3½ oz mixed green leaves with beets strips

PANTRY

8 teaspoons balsamic vinegar; black pepper

Seared Chicken Sandwich

■ Put the mini chicken breast fillets into a plastic bag with half the vinegar and toss together until evenly coated.

■ Heat a nonstick skillet, lift the chicken out of the bag with a fork and add the pieces to the pan. Cook for 3 minutes, turn and drizzle with the vinegar from the bag and cook for 2–3 more minutes or until browned and cooked through.

■ Toast the bread lightly. Slice the chicken into long, thin strips and arrange them on 4 slices of toast. Mix together the yogurt and horseradish and a little pepper to taste. Add the greens and toss together.

■ Spoon the yogurt and salad greens over the chicken, drizzle over the remaining vinegar, if desired, and top with the remaining slices of toast. Cut each sandwich in half and serve immediately.

ADD A GARLIC KICK

Toss the chicken fillets with the juice of ½ lemon and 1 tablespoon olive oil then sauté as in the main recipe but without the vinegar. Toast 8 slices wholewheat bread then spread with ¼ cup garlic mayonnaise. Divide the chicken between 4 slices of toast then top with the shredded leaves of 2 Little Gem lettuces and a 2 inch piece of cucumber, thinly sliced. Cover with the remaining slices of toast then press together and cut into triangles. Calories per serving 380

SERVES 4

Calories per serving 200
Preparation time 10 minutes, plus standing

INGREDIENTS

1	2 (13 oz) cans chickpeas, drained and rinsed
2	4 tomatoes, diced
3	handful of herbs (such as mint and parsley), chopped
4	pinch of paprika
5	pinch of ground cumin

PANTRY

1 red onion, finely sliced, ¼ cup lemon juice;
1 tablespoon olive oil; salt and black pepper

Moroccan Chickpea Salad

■ Mix together all the ingredients in a large nonmetallic bowl. Set aside for 10 minutes to allow the flavors to infuse, then serve.

SERVES 4

Calories per serving 257
Preparation time 10 minutes
Cooking time 3 minutes

INGREDIENTS

1	**8 oz wild strawberries, hulled**
2	**12 king scallops, without corals, cut into 3 slices**
3	**3 leeks, cut into matchstick-thin strips**
4	**8 oz mixed green leaves**
5	**12 wild strawberries or 5 larger strawberries, chopped, plus 8 wild strawberries or 3 larger strawberries halved, to garnish**

PANTRY

2 tablespoons balsamic vinegar; 1 tablespoon lemon juice, plus juice of 1 lemon; 2½ fl oz olive oil; salt and black pepper

Warm Scallop Salad

■ Put the hulled strawberries, vinegar, 1 tablespoon lemon juice, and 2 fl oz of the oil in a food processor or blender and process until smooth. Pass through a fine sieve or cloth to remove seeds and set aside.

■ Season the scallops with salt and pepper and the remaining lemon juice.

■ Prepare the garnish. Heat the remaining oil in a nonstick skillet, add the leeks and cook over high heat, stirring, for 1 minute or until golden brown. Remove and set aside.

■ Add the scallop slices to the pan and cook for 20–30 seconds each side. Divide the green leaves across 4 serving plates. Arrange the scallop slices over the salad.

■ Heat the strawberry mixture gently in a small saucepan for 20–30 seconds, then pour over the scallops and greens. Sprinkle the leeks on top and garnish with the halved strawberries. Season with a little pepper and serve.

ADD A DRESSING

Whisk together 2 tablespoons extra virgin olive oil, 1 teaspoon sesame oil, 1 tablespoon light soy sauce, 2 teaspoons balsamic vinegar, 1 teaspoon honey, and pepper to taste in a bowl. Cook the scallops as in the main recipe (omitting the leeks) and arrange over the greens. Heat the dressing gently as in the main recipe, then pour over the scallops and salad. Calories per serving 173

SERVES 4

Calories per serving 250 (excluding walnut bread)
Preparation time 10 minutes, plus cooling
Cooking time 10 minutes

INGREDIENTS

| 1 | 3 red bell peppers, halved, cored, and seeded |

| 2 | 1 red chile, seeded and sliced |

| 3 | 3 oz Polish sausage, thinly sliced |

| 4 | 2 (13½ oz) cans butter or flageolet beans, rinsed and drained |

| 5 | 2 tablespoons chopped fresh cilantro |

PANTRY

1 tablespoon olive oil; 1 onion, sliced; 1 tablespoon balsamic vinegar

Bean, Polish Sausage, & Pepper Salad

■ Put the peppers on a baking sheet, skin side up, and cook under a preheated hot broiler for 8–10 minutes until the skins are blackened. Cover with damp paper towel. When the peppers are cool enough to handle, remove the skins and slice the flesh.

■ Meanwhile heat the oil in a nonstick skillet, add the onion and sauté for 5–6 minutes until soft. Add the sausage and cook for 1–2 minutes until crisp.

■ Mix together the beans and balsamic vinegar, then add the onion and sausage mixture and the peppers and chile.

A VEGETARIAN VERSION

Omit the sausage and mix 2 oz halved pitted black olives with the beans. Slice and grill 3 oz haloumi. Divide the salad among bowls and top with the haloumi. Calories per serving 248

SERVES 4

Calories per serving 99
Preparation time 10 minutes
Cooking time 2 minutes

INGREDIENTS

1	1 tablespoon black sesame seeds
2	1 lb watermelon, peeled, seeded, and diced
3	6 oz feta cheese, diced
4	2½ handfuls of arugula
5	handful of mint

PANTRY

2 tablespoons olive oil; juice of ½ large lemon; salt and black pepper

Watermelon & Feta Salad

■ Dry-fry the sesame seeds for a few minutes until aromatic, then set aside. Arrange the watermelon and feta on a large serving plate with the arugula and mint.

■ Whisk together the olive oil and lemon juice, then season to taste with salt and pepper. Drizzle over the salad, sprinkle with the sesame seeds and serve.

SERVES 6

Calories per serving 186
Preparation time 20 minutes
Cooking time 25 minutes

INGREDIENTS

1 12 oz, or 3 small, different colored bell peppers

2 1 lb tomatoes, skinned, seeded, and chopped

3 6 large eggs

4 thyme sprigs, leaves removed, or large pinch of dried thyme, plus extra sprigs to garnish

5 4 oz pastrami, thinly sliced

PANTRY

2 tablespoons olive oil; salt and black pepper; 1 onion, finely chopped; 2 garlic cloves, crushed

Piperade with Pastrami

■ Make the sofrito. Put the peppers on a baking sheet, skin side up, and cook under a preheated hot broiler for 8–10 minutes until the skins are blackened. Cover with damp paper towel. When the peppers are cool enough to handle, remove the skins, seed, and cut the flesh into strips.

■ Heat 1 tablespoon of the the oil in a large skillet, add the onion and cook gently for 10 minutes until softened and transparent. Add the garlic, tomatoes, and peppers and simmer for 5 minutes until all the juices have evaporated from the tomatoes. Set aside until ready to serve.

■ Beat the eggs together with the thyme and salt and pepper in a bowl. Reheat the sofrito. Heat the remaining oil in a saucepan, add the eggs, stirring until they are lightly scrambled. Stir into the reheated sofrito and spoon onto plates.

■ Arrange slices of pastrami around the eggs and serve immediately, garnished with a little extra thyme.

Calories per serving 190
Preparation time 15 minutes, plus marinating
Cooking time 3 minutes

INGREDIENTS

1	**1 (13 oz) can borlotti beans, drained and rinsed**
2	**1 red chile, seeded and finely chopped**
3	**2 celery sticks, thinly sliced**
4	**1 (7 oz) can tuna in olive oil, drained and flaked**
5	**2 oz arugula**

PANTRY

1 tablespoon water (optional); 2 tablespoons extra virgin olive oil; 2 garlic cloves, crushed; ½ red onion, cut into thin wedges; finely grated zest and juice of 1 lemon; salt and black pepper

Tuna & Borlotti Bean Salad

■ Heat the borlotti beans in a saucepan over medium heat for 3 minutes, adding the measured water if starting to stick to the base.

■ Put the oil, garlic, and chile in a large bowl. Stir in the celery, onion, and hot beans and season with salt and pepper. Cover and let marinate at room temperature for at least 30 minutes and up to 4 hours.

■ Stir in the tuna and lemon zest and juice. Gently toss in the arugula, taste and adjust the seasoning with extra salt, pepper, and lemon juice, if necessary.

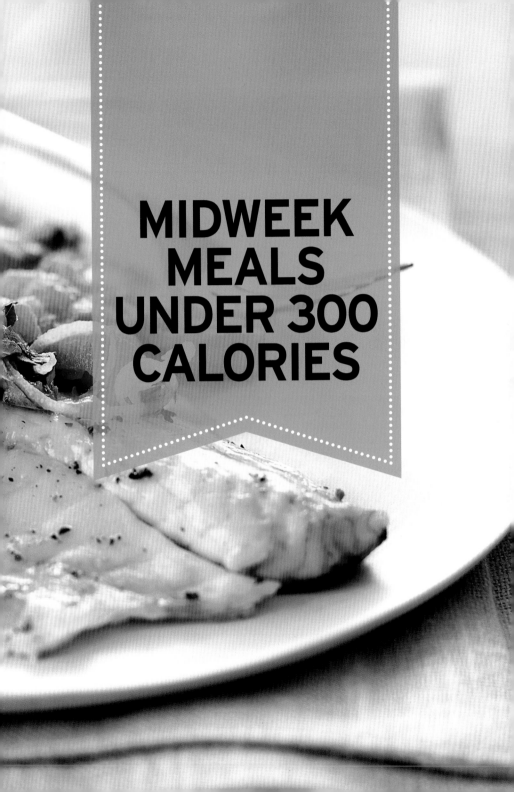

MIDWEEK MEALS UNDER 300 CALORIES

SERVES 4

Calories per serving 239
Preparation time 5 minutes
Cooking time 15 minutes

INGREDIENTS

1 | 8 oz cherry tomatoes, halved

2 | 3½ oz pitted black olives

3 | 2 tablespoons capers in brine, drained

4 | 2 tablespoons finely chopped fresh mixed herbs, including thyme and parsley

5 | 4 cod fillets, about 6 oz each

PANTRY

2 tablespoons extra virgin olive oil; 2 tablespoons balsamic vinegar; salt and black pepper

Baked Cod with Tomatoes & Olives

■ Combine the tomatoes, olives, capers, and herbs in a roasting pan. Nestle the cod fillets in the pan, drizzle over the oil and balsamic vinegar, and season to taste with salt and pepper.

■ Bake in a preheated oven, at 400°F, for 15 minutes.

■ Transfer the fish, tomatoes, and olives to warm plates. Spoon the pan juices over the fish. Serve immediately.

Calories per serving 197
Preparation time 10 minutes
Cooking time 16–20 minutes

INGREDIENTS

1	**8 boneless chicken thighs**
2	**2 tablespoons Dijon mustard**
3	**6 drops Tabasco sauce**
4	**1 tablespoon soy sauce**
5	**greens, to serve**

PANTRY

2 garlic cloves, crushed

Deviled Chicken

■ Heat a large ridged grill pan (or ordinary skillet).

■ Remove the skin from the chicken thighs, open them out and trim away any excess fat.

■ To make the devil sauce, mix together the mustard, Tabasco, garlic, and soy sauce in a shallow dish.

■ Dip the trimmed chicken thighs in the devil sauce and coat each piece well. Place the chicken pieces flat on the pan and cook in 2 batches for 8–10 minutes on each side.

■ Serve hot or cold with salad.

HOT CHICKEN

Mix 3 tablespoons jerk marinade (a ready-made paste) with the grated zest and juice of ½ an orange and 2 finely chopped cloves of garlic. Dip the chicken in this mixture then cook as in the main recipe. Serve with rice or a salad. Calories per serving 193

SERVES 4

Calories per serving 268
Preparation time 10 minutes
Cooking time 20–25 minutes

INGREDIENTS

1   2 tablespoons medium curry paste

2   3 lb prepared mixed vegetables (such as zucchini, pepper, mushrooms, green beans and potato—no more than 1 lb potato)

3   1 (7 oz) can diced tomatoes

4   1 (13 oz) can low-fat coconut milk

5   2 tablespoons chopped cilantro leaves

PANTRY

1 tablespoon olive oil; 1 onion, chopped; 1 garlic clove, crushed

Vegetable Curry

■ Heat the oil in a large saucepan, add the onion and garlic and sauté for 2 minutes. Stir in the curry paste and continue cooking for 1 minute more.

■ Add the vegetables and cook for 2–3 minutes, stirring occasionally, then add the canned tomatoes and coconut milk. Stir well, bring to a boil, then lower the heat and simmer for 12–15 minutes until all the vegetables are cooked.

■ Stir in the cilantro and serve.

SERVES 4

Calories per serving 230
Preparation time 20 minutes
Cooking time 25–30 minutes

INGREDIENTS

1	13 oz raw beets, peeled and diced
2	1¼ lb pumpkin or butternut squash, peeled, seeded, and cut into slightly larger dice
3	2 teaspoons fennel seeds
4	2 small goat cheeses, 3½ oz each
5	chopped rosemary, to garnish

PANTRY

1 red onion, cut into wedges; 2 tablespoons olive oil; salt and black pepper

Pumpkin & Goat Cheese Casserole

■ Put the beetst, pumpkin, and onion into a roasting pan, drizzle with the oil, and sprinkle with the fennel seeds and salt and pepper. Roast the vegetables in a preheated oven, at 400°F, for 20–25 minutes, turning once, until browned and tender.

■ Cut the goat cheeses in half and nestle each half among the roasted vegetables. Sprinkle them with a little salt and pepper and drizzle with some of the pan juices.

■ Return the dish to the oven for about 5 minutes more, until the cheese is just beginning to melt. Sprinkle with rosemary and serve immediately.

SERVES 4

Calories per serving 237
Preparation time 10 minutes
Cooking time 30 minutes

INGREDIENTS

1	8 plum tomatoes, halved
2	4 sea bass fillets, about 5 oz each
3	2 tablespoons chopped basil, plus leaves to garnish

PANTRY

2 tablespoons juice and grated zest of 1 lemon, plus wedges to garnish; 2 tablespoons extra virgin olive oil; salt and black pepper

Bass with Tomato & Basil Sauce

■ Make the sauce up to 2 days in advance. Arrange the tomatoes in a roasting pan, season well and cook in a preheated oven, at 400°F, for 20 minutes.

■ Transfer the tomatoes and any cooking juices to a pan and heat through gently with the lemon juice and most of the zest. Season to taste and set aside until ready to serve.

■ Season the fish fillets and cook under a preheated hot broiler for approximately 10 minutes or until the fish is cooked through.

■ Meanwhile, warm the sauce through. Stir the chopped basil and oil into the sauce and spoon it over the fish. Garnish with basil leaves, the rest of the lemon zest, and lemon wedges.

SWITCH TO SHRIMP

Replace the bass fillets with 16 raw, peeled jumbo shrimp. Fry the shrimp in a little oil spray until pink and cooked through. Make the sauce as in the main recipe and spoon over the top of the cooked shrimp to serve. Calories per serving 169

SERVES 4

Calories per serving 282
Preparation time 10 minutes
Cooking time 20-25 minutes

INGREDIENTS

1	2 tablespoons butter or margarine
2	7 oz wild mushrooms, trimmed and sliced
3	8 large eggs, beaten
4	2 tablespoons chopped parsley
5	2 oz Gruyère cheese, grated

PANTRY

black pepper

Wild Mushroom Omelet

■ Melt a little of the butter or margarine in an omelet pan, add the mushrooms and sauté for 5-6 minutes until cooked and any moisture has evaporated. Remove the mushrooms from the pan.

■ Melt a little more butter or margarine in the same pan and add one-quarter of the beaten egg. Season well with pepper and stir with a wooden spoon, bringing the cooked egg to the center of the pan and allowing the runny egg to flow to the edge of the pan and cook.

■ When there is only a little liquid egg left, sprinkle over a quarter of the mushrooms and some of the parsley and Gruyère. Fold the omelet over, tip onto a warm serving plate and keep warm while you make 3 more omelets in the same way.

Calories per serving 248
Preparation time 10 minutes
Cooking time 25–30 minutes

INGREDIENTS

| 1 | 14½ oz peeled butternut squash, diced |

| 2 | 8 eggs |

| 3 | 1 tablespoon chopped thyme |

| 4 | 2 tablespoons chopped sage |

| 5 | 4 oz ricotta cheese |

PANTRY

1 tablespoon extra virgin rapeseed oil; 1 red onion, thinly sliced; salt and black pepper

Butternut Squash & Ricotta Frittata

■ Heat the oil in a large, deep skillet with an ovenproof handle over medium-low heat, add the onion and butternut squash, then cover loosely and cook gently, stirring frequently, for 18–20 minutes or until softened and golden.

■ Lightly beat the eggs, thyme, sage, and ricotta in a bowl, season the mixture well with salt and pepper and pour over the butternut squash.

■ Cook for an additional 2–3 minutes until the egg is almost set, stirring occasionally with a heat-resistant rubber spatula to prevent the base from burning.

■ Slide the pan under a preheated broiler, keeping the handle away from the heat, and grill for 3–4 minutes or until the egg is set and the frittata is golden. Slice into 6 wedges and serve hot.

SERVES 4

Calories per serving 136
Preparation time 5 minutes
Cooking time 15 minutes

INGREDIENTS

1   2 strips smoked bacon, chopped

2   a few sprigs of thyme or lemon thyme

3   2 (13 oz) cans cannellini beans, drained and rinsed

4   2 tablespoons chopped parsley

PANTRY

1 teaspoon olive oil; 2 garlic cloves, crushed; 1 onion, chopped; 1½ pints vegetable stock; black pepper

Bacon & White Bean Soup

■ Heat the oil in a large saucepan, then add the bacon, garlic, and onion and fry for 3–4 minutes until the bacon is beginning to brown and the onion to soften.

■ Add the thyme and continue to fry for 1 minute. Then add the beans and stock to the pan, bring to a boil and simmer for 10 minutes.

■ Transfer the soup to a liquidizer or food processor and blend with the parsley and pepper until smooth.

■ Return to the pan and heat through to serve.

SERVES 4

Calories per serving 149
Preparation time 10 minutes
Cooking time 15 minutes

INGREDIENTS

1	4 chicken thighs, skinned and boned
2	2 tablespoons honey
3	2 tablespoons mild wholegrain mustard
4	1 zucchini, cut into 8 large pieces
5	1 carrot, cut into 8 large pieces

Chicken & Vegetable Skewers

■ Cut the chicken thighs into bite-sized pieces and toss in the honey and mustard. Arrange the chicken pieces on a baking sheet and bake in a preheated oven, at 350°F, for 15 minutes until cooked through and lightly golden. Set aside and let cool.

■ Take 8 bamboo skewers and thread with the cooked chicken pieces and the raw vegetables.

■ Serve with the honey and mustard mixture for dipping. The skewers can also be refrigerated for adding to the following day's lunchbox.

ADD A STICKY GLAZE

Mix together 2 tablespoons ketchup, 2 teaspoons honey, 2 finely chopped cloves of garlic, and 1 tablespoon of sunflower oil. Dip the chicken into the ketchup mixture then cook as in the main recipe. Thread onto skewers with 1 red pepper, seeded, cored, and cut into chunks and 8 cherry tomatoes. Calories per serving 158

SERVES 4

Calories per serving 187 (excluding potatoes or pasta)
Preparation time 5 minutes
Cooking time 10 minutes

INGREDIENTS

1	1 tablespoon unsalted butter
2	2 oz pancetta or smoked bacon, finely chopped
3	1 lb raw, peeled jumbo shrimp
4	1 large bunch of watercress

PANTRY

1 teaspoon olive oil; grated zest and juice of 1 lemon

Jumbo Shrimp with Pancetta

■ Heat the oil and butter in a large skillet, add the pancetta or smoked bacon and fry for 3–4 minutes until crisp.

■ Add the shrimp and fry for 1 minute on each side. Sprinkle over the lemon zest and juice and continue to fry for 1 minute, then add the watercress and combine well.

■ Serve as a small lunch or with potatoes or pasta as a larger main course.

Calories per serving 216
Preparation time 10 minutes
Cooking time 5 minutes

INGREDIENTS

1	**1½ tablespoons ready-made or homemade Thai red curry paste**
2	**12 oz lean pork, sliced into thin strips**
3	**7 oz French beans, topped and cut in half**
4	**2 tablespoons Thai fish sauce (nampla)**
5	**Chinese chives or regular chives, to garnish**

PANTRY

2 tablespoons groundnut oil; 1 teaspoon sugar

Thai Red Pork & Bean Curry

■ Heat the oil in a wok over medium heat until the oil starts to shimmer. Add the curry paste and cook, stirring, until it releases its aroma.

■ Add the pork and French beans and stir-fry for 2–3 minutes until the meat is cooked through and the beans are just tender.

■ Stir in the fish sauce and sugar and serve, garnished with chives.

SERVES 6

Calories per serving 218
Preparation time 10 minutes
Cooking time 15–20 minutes

INGREDIENTS

| 1 | 4 oz orzo, macaroni, or other small pasta shapes |

| 2 | 2 tablespoons butter |

| 3 | 4 egg yolks |

| 4 | 4 oz cooked chicken, torn into fine shreds |

| 5 | oregano leaves |

PANTRY

3½ pints chicken stock; ¼ cup flour; grated zest and juice of 1 lemon, plus extra lemon zest and lemon wedges; salt and black pepper

Greek Chicken Avgolomeno

■ Bring the stock to a boil, add the pasta and simmer for 8–10 minutes until just tender.

■ Meanwhile, heat the butter in a separate smaller pan, stir in the flour then gradually mix in 2 ladlefuls of the stock from the large pan. Bring to a boil, stirring. Take off the heat.

■ Mix the egg yolks in a medium-sized bowl with the lemon zest and some salt and pepper. Gradually mix in the lemon juice until smooth. Slowly mix in the hot sauce from the small pan, stirring continuously.

■ Stir a couple more hot ladlefuls of stock into the lemon mixture once the pasta is cooked, then pour this into the large pasta pan. (Don't be tempted to add the eggs and lemon straight into the pasta pan or it may curdle.) Mix well, then ladle into shallow soup bowls and top with the chicken, some extra lemon zest and some torn oregano leaves. Serve with lemon wedges.

SERVES 4

Calories per serving 160
Preparation time 15 minutes
Cooking time 25 minutes

INGREDIENTS

1   **4 lean bacon strips, chopped**

2   **1 lb sweet potatoes, chopped**

3   **2 parsnips, chopped**

4   **1 teaspoon chopped thyme**

5   **1 baby Savoy cabbage, shredded**

STOCK CUPBOARD

2 onions, chopped; 2 garlic cloves, sliced; 1½ pints
vegetable stock

Sweet Potato & Cabbage Soup

■ Place the onions, garlic, and bacon in a
large saucepan and sauté for 2–3 minutes.

■ Add the sweet potatoes, parsnips,
thyme and stock, bring to a boil and
simmer for 15 minutes.

■ Transfer two-thirds of the soup to a
liquidizer or food processor and blend
until smooth. Return to the pan, add the
cabbage and continue to simmer for 5–7
minutes until the cabbage is just cooked.

TRY IT WITH BROCCOLI

Follow the main recipe, replacing the sweet potatoes with 1 lb peeled and chopped butternut squash. After returning the blended soup to the pan, add 3½ oz broccoli, broken into small florets. Cook as in the main recipe, omitting the cabbage. Calories per serving 160

SERVES 6

Calories per serving 122
Preparation time 5 minutes
Cooking time 10 minutes

INGREDIENTS

1 2 lb large, uncooked langoustines in their shells (thawed if frozen)

2 1½ inch piece of fresh ginger, peeled and finely chopped

3 2 teaspoons tamarind paste

4 juice of 2 limes and lime wedges

5 small bunch of cilantro, torn into pieces

PANTRY

2 tablespoons olive oil; 1 large onion, chopped; 3–4 garlic cloves, finely chopped; ½ pint fish stock

Langoustines with Tamarind & Lime

■ Rinse the langoustines in cold water and drain well. Heat the oil in a large saucepan or wok, add the onion and sauté for 5 minutes until just beginning to brown.

■ Stir in the garlic, ginger, and tamarind paste, then mix in the lime juice and stock.

■ Bring the stock to a boil, add the langoustines and cook, stirring, for 5 minutes until the langoustines are bright pink. Spoon into bowls and serve garnished with the torn cilantro leaves and lime wedges.

SERVES 6

Calories per serving 107
Preparation time 15 minutes
Cooking time 25 minutes

INGREDIENTS

1	¼ pint marsala or sweet sherry
2	1 vanilla pod
3	6 peaches, halved and pitted
4	5 oz fresh raspberries

PANTRY

8 fl oz water; ⅓ cup sugar

Poached Peaches & Raspberries

■ Pour the water and marsala or sherry into a saucepan and add the sugar. Slit the vanilla pod lengthwise and scrape out the black seeds from inside the pod. Add these to the water with the pod, then gently heat the mixture until the sugar has dissolved.

■ Place the peach halves, cut side down, in an overproof dish so that they sit together snugly. Pour over the hot syrup, then cover and cook in a preheated oven, at 350°F, for 20 minutes.

■ Sprinkle with the raspberries. Serve the fruit either warm or cold. Spoon into serving bowls and decorate with the vanilla pod cut into thin strips.

MIDWEEK MEALS UNDER 500 CALORIES

SERVES 4

Calories per serving 498
Preparation time 10 minutes
Cooking time 10 minutes

INGREDIENTS

1 4 mini pizza bases

2 8 oz reduced-fat mozzarella cheese, shredded

3 8 cherry tomatoes, quartered

4 5 oz prosciutto, sliced

5 2 oz arugula, washed

PANTRY

2 garlic cloves, halved; balsamic vinegar, to taste; salt and black pepper

Quick Prosciutto & Arugula Pizza

■ Rub the top surfaces of the pizza bases with the cut faces of the garlic cloves and discard the cloves.

■ Put the pizza bases on a baking sheet, top with mozzarella and tomatoes and bake in a preheated oven, at 400°F, for 10 minutes until the bread is golden.

■ Top the pizzas with prosciutto and arugula leaves, season to taste with salt, pepper, and balsamic vinegar and serve immediately.

MAKE A HAWAIIAN

Drain and chop 1 (7½ oz) can of pineapple rings, and drain and flake 1 (5½ oz) can tuna in spring water. Top the pizza bases with the pineapple and tuna then sprinkle over the mozzarella and tomatoes before cooking as in the main recipe. Calories per serving 481

Calories per serving 340
Preparation time 5 minutes, plus marinating
Cooking time 5-6 minutes

INGREDIENTS

1 **4 boneless, skinless chicken breasts, about 1 lb in total, cut into 1 inch cubes**

2 **¼ cup dark soy sauce, plus extra to serve**

3 **¼ cup mirin**

4 **8 oz soba noodles**

PANTRY

2 tablespoons sugar; sesame oil, to serve

Chicken Teriyaki

■ Place the chicken in a shallow dish. Combine the soy sauce, mirin, and sugar, add to the chicken and toss well to coat. Set aside to marinate for 15 minutes.

■ Meanwhile, cook the noodles according to the package instructions, then drain, refresh in iced water, drain again and chill.

■ Thread the chicken cubes onto metal skewers and barbecue or grill for 2–3 minutes on each side.

■ Toss the noodles with a little sesame oil and serve with the chicken and extra sesame oil and soy sauce.

Calories per serving 353
Preparation time 5 minutes
Cooking time 5 minutes

INGREDIENTS

1   **3 sirloin steaks, about 10 oz each**

2   **5 oz radicchio, sliced into 1 inch strips**

PANTRY

½ tablespoon olive oil; 2 garlic cloves, finely
chopped; salt

Beef Strips with Radicchio

■ Trim the fat from the steaks and slice the
meat into very thin strips.

■ Heat the oil in a heavy skillet over high
heat, add the garlic and steak strips, season
with salt and stir-fry for 2 minutes or until
the steak strips are golden brown.

■ Add the radicchio and stir-fry until
the leaves are just beginning to wilt.
Serve immediately.

SERVES 4

Calories per serving 357
Preparation time 15 minutes
Cooking time 45 minutes

INGREDIENTS

| 1 | 4 × 4 oz boneless, skinless chicken breasts |

| 2 | 2 red bell peppers, cored, seeded, and cut into flat pieces |

| 3 | 1 bunch asparagus, trimmed |

| 4 | 7 oz new potatoes, boiled, cut in half |

| 5 | 1 bunch basil |

PANTRY

2 small red onions; 5 tablespoons olive oil; 2 tablespoons balsamic vinegar; salt and black pepper

Grilled Summer Chicken Salad

■ Heat a ridged grill pan (or ordinary skillet). Place the chicken breasts in the pan and cook for 8–10 minutes on each side. When cooked, remove from the pan and cut into chunks.

■ Cut the red onions into wedges, keeping the root ends intact to hold the wedges together. Place in the pan and cook for 5 minutes on each side. Remove from the pan and set aside.

■ Place the flat pieces of red pepper in the pan and cook for 8 minutes on the skin side only, so that the skins are charred and blistered. Remove and set aside, then cook the asparagus in the pan for 6 minutes, turning frequently.

■ Put the boiled potatoes in a large bowl. Tear the basil, keeping a few leaves intact to garnish, and add to the bowl, together with the chicken and all the vegetables. Add the olive oil, balsamic vinegar, and seasoning. Toss the salad and garnish with the reserved basil leaves.

SERVES 2

Calories per serving 393
Preparation time 10 minutes
Cooking time 12–16 minutes

INGREDIENTS

1	¾ lb potatoes, peeled and cubed
2	3 tablespoons light sour cream
3	½ tablespoon chopped sage
4	2 slices of calves liver, about 5 oz each
5	gravy, to serve

PANTRY

1 garlic clove; 1 tablespoon seasoned flour;
2 tablespoons olive oil; salt and black pepper

Calves' Liver with Mashed Potato

■ Cook the potatoes and garlic in a saucepan of lightly salted boiling water for 10–12 minutes until tender, then drain. Return the potatoes and garlic to the pan and mash with the sour cream and sage. Season well with pepper.

■ Meanwhile, press the pieces of liver into the seasoned flour to coat them all over. Heat the oil in a skillet, add the liver and fry for 1–2 minutes on each side or until cooked to your liking. Serve with the mashed potatoes and gravy.

SERVES 4

Calories per serving 350
Preparation time 5 minutes
Cooking time 30 minutes

INGREDIENTS

1   4 red bell peppers, halved, cored, and seeded, with stems left on

2   1 (13 oz) can flageolet beans, drained and rinsed

3   4 oz firm goat cheese

4   8 teaspoons ready-made pesto

PANTRY

4 teaspoons olive oil

Grilled Peppers with Goat Cheese

■ Put the pepper halves on a baking sheet, skin side down, and divide the flageolet beans among them. Drizzle with the oil.

■ Cut the goat cheese horizontally into 8 slices and arrange the slices on top of the beans. Top each stack with 1 teaspoon pesto.

■ Cover the peppers with foil and bake in a preheated oven, at 400°F, for 20 minutes or until the peppers are tender. Remove the foil and bake for another 10 minutes.

SERVES 4

Calories per serving 461
Preparation time 10 minutes
Cooking time about 10 minutes

INGREDIENTS

| 1 | 7 oz chorizo sausage, cut into ½ inch dice |

| 2 | 2 ripe tomatoes, seeded, and finely diced |

| 3 | 3 tablespoons chopped parsley |

| 4 | 2 (13 oz) cans chickpeas, drained |

PANTRY

2 tablespoons olive oil; 1 red onion, finely chopped;
2 garlic cloves, crushed; salt and black pepper

Chickpeas with Chorizo

■ Heat the oil in a large nonstick skillet,
add the onion, garlic, and chorizo and cook
over medium-high heat, stirring frequently,
for 4–5 minutes.

■ Add the tomatoes, parsley, and
chickpeas to the pan and cook, stirring
frequently, for 4–5 minutes or until the
mixture is heated through.

■ Season to taste with salt and pepper
and serve immediately or let cool to room
temperature.

Calories per serving 451
Preparation time 10 minutes
Cooking time 15 minutes

INGREDIENTS

| 1 | 1 lb small new potatoes, scrubbed |

| 2 | 4 fresh tuna steaks, about 6 oz each |

| 3 | 3½ oz baby spinach leaves, roughly chopped |

| 4 | grilled lime wedges, to serve |

PANTRY

¼ cup olive oil; 2 tablespoons balsamic vinegar; salt and black pepper

Grilled Tuna Salad

■ Place the new potatoes in a steamer over boiling water and cook for 15 minutes or until tender.

■ Meanwhile, heat a ridged grill pan. Pat the tuna fillets dry with paper towel, and cook in the pan for 3 minutes on each side for rare, 5 minutes for medium, or 8 minutes for well done.

■ Remove the potatoes from the steamer. Slice them in half and place in a bowl. Add the spinach, olive oil, and balsamic vinegar. Toss and season to taste. Divide the salad between 4 plates and serve with a slice of tuna arranged on the top of each, and a grilled lime wedge for squeezing.

SERVES 4

Calories per serving 413
Preparation time 5 minutes
Cooking time 20–25 minutes

INGREDIENTS

1   ¼ cup medium curry paste

2   8 boneless, skinless chicken thighs, cut into thin strips

3   1 (13 oz) can diced tomatoes

4   8 oz broccoli, broken into small florets, stems peeled and sliced

5   3½ fl oz coconut milk

PANTRY

3 tablespoons olive oil; 1 onion, finely chopped; salt and black pepper

Fast Chicken Curry

■ Heat the oil in a deep nonstick saucepan over medium heat. Add the onion and cook for 3 minutes until soft and translucent. Add the curry paste and cook, stirring, for 1 minute until fragrant.

■ Add the chicken, tomatoes, and coconut milk to the pan. Bring to a boil, then reduce the heat, cover and simmer gently over low heat for 15–20 minutes, adding the broccoli after 10 minutes, until the chicken is cooked through.

■ Remove from the heat, season well with salt and pepper and serve immediately.

Calories per serving 422
Preparation time 10 minutes
Cooking time 10 minutes

INGREDIENTS

| 1 | 4 trout fillets, about 7 oz each |

| 2 | large handful of basil, coarsely chopped, plus extra to garnish |

| 3 | 2 oz Parmesan cheese, freshly grated |

| 4 | salad, to serve |

PANTRY

¼ cup olive oil, plus extra for greasing;
1 garlic clove, crushed; salt and black pepper

Trout with Pesto

■ Brush a foil-lined baking sheet lightly with oil and place under a preheated very hot broiler to heat up.

■ Put the trout fillets onto the hot sheet, sprinkle with salt and pepper and place under the broiler for 8–10 minutes until lightly browned and the fish flakes easily when pressed with a knife.

■ Meanwhile, put the basil and garlic into a bowl. Work in the oil using a handheld blender. Stir in the Parmesan cheese.

■ Remove the fish from the broiler, transfer to serving plates, drizzle with the pesto, sprinkle with extra basil leaves to garnish, and serve with salad.

A FRUITY VERSION

Put the trout fillets on a foil-lined broiler pan as in the main recipe. Mix together the finely grated zest and juice of 1 small orange, 1 tablespoon chopped parsley, and ¼ cup olive oil. Brush the mixture over the fillets and season with salt and pepper. Broil until golden and opaque, then sprinkle with toasted flaked almonds. Serve with a simple salad. Calories per serving 403

SERVES 4

Calories per serving 401
Preparation time 10 minutes, plus marinating
Cooking time 16–20 minutes

INGREDIENTS

1 4 (4 oz) boneless, skinless chicken breasts

2 ¼ cup tandoori paste or powder

3 4 tomatoes, finely sliced

4 1 bunch fresh cilantro, coarsely chopped

PANTRY

2 red onions, finely sliced; ¼ cup lemon juice, plus lemon wedges, grilled (optional), to serve; ¼ cup olive oil; salt and black pepper

Grilled Tandoori Chicken

■ Using a sharp knife, make a series of small slashes in the flesh of the chicken breasts and rub in the tandoori paste or powder. Leave to marinate in the refrigerator overnight.

■ Heat a ridged grill pan (or ordinary skillet). Cook the marinated chicken breasts for 8–10 minutes on each side, allowing the authentic tandoori charred color to appear, until cooked throroughly.

■ Mix the red onions, tomatoes, and cilantro together with the lemon juice, olive oil and seasoning in a small bowl. Serve the salad with the tandoori chicken, accompanied by lemon wedges, grilled if desired.

TRY HARISSA

Rub the slashed chicken with 4
teaspoons harissa paste instead
of the tandoori paste or powder.
Marinate then fry. Soak 7 oz couscous
in ¾ pint boiling water for 5 minutes.
Stir in 2 tablespoons olive oil, 3
tablespoons fresh chopped cilantro,
and seasoning. Serve with lemon
wedges. Calories per serving 402

SERVES 2

Calories per serving 417
Preparation time 10 minutes
Cooking time 15 minutes

INGREDIENTS

| 1 | 1 (13 oz) can butter beans, drained and rinsed |

| 2 | 7 oz baby spinach leaves |

| 3 | 4 eggs, beaten |

| 4 | 2 oz ricotta cheese |

PANTRY

1 teaspoon olive oil; 1 onion, sliced; salt and black pepper (optional)

Spinach & Ricotta Frittata

■ Heat the oil in a medium skillet, add the onion and sauté for 3–4 minutes until softened. Add the butter beans and spinach and heat gently for 2–3 minutes until the spinach has wilted.

■ Pour in the eggs, then spoon in the ricotta and season with salt and pepper if desired. Cook until almost set, then place the pan under a hot broiler and cook for another 1–2 minutes until golden and set.

SERVES 6

Calories per serving 476
Preparation time 15 minutes
Cooking time 1¾–2¼ hours

INGREDIENTS

1	**12 large chicken drumsticks**
2	**6 tablespoons very finely chopped lemon grass**
3	**1 lemon grass stalk, halved lengthwise**
4	**1 red chile, finely sliced or chopped**
5	**2 tablespoons medium curry paste**

PANTRY

1 tablespoon sunflower oil; 1 onion, finely chopped; 4 garlic cloves, crushed; 1 tablespoon granulated palm sugar; 8 fl oz chicken stock; salt and black pepper

Lemon Grass Chicken

■ Heat the oil in a large, heavy casserole dish and brown the drumsticks evenly for 5–6 minutes. Remove with a slotted spoon and set aside.

■ Add the onion and stir-fry over low heat for 10 minutes. Add the garlic, lemon grass, chile and curry paste and stir-fry for 1–2 minutes.

■ Return the chicken to the dish with the palm sugar and stock. Bring to a boil, season, and cover tightly. Cook in a preheated oven, at 275°F, for 1½–2 hours or until tender. Remove from the oven and serve immediately.

SERVES 4

Calories per serving 435
Preparation time: 10–15 minutes
Cooking time: 35 minutes

INGREDIENTS

1   **4 red bell peppers, cored, seeded, and sliced**

2   **2½ oz walnuts, chopped**

3   **10 oz fresh egg pappardelle**

4   **1 oz Parmesan cheese shavings**

PANTRY

2 teaspoons olive oil; 3–4 large garlic cloves, thinly sliced; salt and black pepper

Pepper & Walnut Pappardelle

■ Put the peppers on a baking sheet, skin side up. Brush with ½ teaspoon of the olive oil and cook under a preheated hot broiler until the skins start to blacken. Cover with damp paper towel. When the peppers are cool enough to handle, remove the skins.

■ Reserve 4 slices of pepper to use as a garnish and dice the remaining peppers.

■ Heat the remaining olive oil in a large skillet over medium-low heat, add the sliced garlic but do not let it brown. Add the diced red pepper and stir in the walnuts. Keep warm.

■ Bring a large saucepan of lightly salted water to a boil. Add the pasta, return to a boil and cook according to the package directions for 3–4 minutes or until al dente. Drain and transfer to a large, warm serving bowl.

■ Toss the pasta well with the garlic, pepper, and walnut mixture. Sprinkle over the Parmesan shavings and garnish with the reserved pepper slices.

Calories per serving 428
Preparation time 10 minutes
Cooking time 25 minutes

INGREDIENTS

1	**10 oz risotto rice**

2	**¼ pint dry white wine**

3	**4 oz light cream cheese**

4	**4 oz smoked salmon, chopped**

5	**¼ cup chopped herbs (such as chives, parsley, or dill)**

PANTRY

2 teaspoons olive oil; 1 onion, finely chopped;
2 garlic cloves, crushed; 1½ pints simmering
vegetable stock; salt and black pepper

Smoked Salmon Risotto

■ Heat the oil in a large saucepan, add the
onion and garlic and sauté for 2–3 minutes
until they begin to soften.

■ Stir in the rice and continue to cook for
1 minute. Add the wine and cook, stirring,
until all the wine has been absorbed.

■ Reduce the heat and add the stock
a little at a time, stirring continuously,
and allowing each amount of stock to be
absorbed before adding the next. Continue
until all the stock has been absorbed.

■ Stir in the cream cheese, smoked
salmon, and herbs, season to taste with salt
and pepper and serve.

SOMETHING
SPECIAL

SERVES 6

Calories per serving 150
Preparation time 10 minutes
Cooking time 6 minutes

INGREDIENTS

1	7 oz trimmed asparagus
2	3 tablespoons chopped hazelnuts
3	1 teaspoon Dijon mustard
4	12 quail eggs
5	8 oz smoked salmon

PANTRY

4 teaspoons olive oil; juice of 1 lemon; salt
and black pepper

Asparagus with Smoked Salmon

■ Put the asparagus in a steamer set over a saucepan of boiling water, cover, and cook for 5 minutes until just tender.

■ Meanwhile, put the nuts in a foil-lined broiler pan and cook under a preheated broiler until lightly browned. In a bowl, lightly mix together the oil, lemon juice, and mustard with a little salt and pepper, then stir in the hot nuts. Keep warm.

■ Pour water into a saucepan to a depth of 1½ inches and bring it to a boil. Lower the eggs into the water with a slotted spoon and cook for 1 minute. Remove the pan from the heat and let the eggs stand for 1 minute. Drain the eggs, then cool under cold running water and drain again.

■ Tear the salmon into strips and divide among 6 serving plates. Do the same with the asparagus, then halve the quail eggs, leaving the shells on if desired, and arrange on top. Drizzle with the warm nut dressing and sprinkle with a little pepper to serve.

SERVES 6

Calories per serving 403
Preparation time 20 minutes
Cooking time 15 minutes

INGREDIENTS

1	3 duck breasts, each about 7½ oz
2	10 oz green beans, trimmed
3	3 clementines, peeled and segmented; plus juice of 2 clementines
4	7 oz spinach or tatsoi

PANTRY

1 tablespoon white wine vinegar; ¼ cup olive oil; salt and black pepper

Duck & Clementine salad

■ Put the duck breasts, skinside down, in a cold ovenproof dish and cook over medium heat for 6 minutes or until the skin has turned crisp and brown. Turn them over and cook for an additional 2 minutes. Transfer the duck to a preheated oven, at 350°F, and cook for 5 minutes until cooked through. Remove the duck breasts from the oven, cover with foil and let rest.

■ Meanwhile, blanch the green beans in lightly salted boiling water for 2 minutes until cooked but still firm and bright green. Drain and refresh in cold water. Transfer the beans to a large salad bowl with the clementine segments.

■ Make the dressing by whisking together the clementine juice, vinegar, and oil in a small bowl. Season to taste with salt and pepper if desired.

■ Add the spinach or tatsoi to the beans and clementines, drizzle over the dressing and combine well. Slice the duck meat, combine it with the salad, and serve immediately.

SERVES 1

Calories per serving 127
Preparation time 15 minutes, plus marinating and chilling
Cooking time 15 minutes

INGREDIENTS

1	**4 oz cod or haddock fillet**
2	**1 tablespoon fresh cilantro leaves**
3	**1 green chile, seeded and chopped**
4	**2 teaspoons natural yogurt**

PANTRY

2 teaspoons lemon juice; 1 garlic clove;
¼ teaspoon sugar

Chile & Cilantro Fish Parcels

■ Place the fish in a nonmetallic dish and sprinkle with the lemon juice. Cover and leave in the refrigerator to marinate for 15–20 minutes.

■ Put the cilantro, garlic, and chile in a food processor or blender and process until the mixture forms a paste. Add the sugar and yogurt and briefly process to blend.

■ Lay the fish on a sheet of foil. Coat the fish on both sides with the paste. Gather up the foil loosely and turn over at the top to seal. Return to the refrigerator for at least 1 hour.

■ Place the parcel on a baking sheet and bake in a preheated oven, at 400°F, for about 15 minutes until the fish is just cooked.

SERVES 4

Calories per serving 444
Preparation time 10 minutes
Cooking time up to 45 minutes

INGREDIENTS

1	**1½ lb loin of venison, cut from the haunch**
2	**2 tablespoons juniper berries, crushed**
3	**1 egg white, lightly beaten**
4	**13 oz green beans**

PANTRY

3 oz mixed peppercorns, crushed; salt
and black pepper

Pepper-crusted Loin of Venison

■ Make sure that the venison fits into your broiler pan; if necessary, cut the loin in half.

■ Combine the peppercorns, juniper berries, and some salt in a shallow dish. Dip the venison in the egg white, roll it in the peppercorn mixture, covering it evenly.

■ Cook the venison under a preheated hot broiler for 4 minutes on each of the four sides, turning it carefully so that the crust stays intact. Transfer the loin to a lightly greased roasting pan and cook in a preheated oven, at 400°F, for another 15 minutes for rare and up to 30 minutes for well done (the time will depend on the thickness of the loin of venison).

■ Let the venison rest for a few minutes, then slice it thickly and serve with green beans and finely sliced sweet potato chips, if desired.

Calories per serving 399
Preparation time 10 minutes
Cooking time 10 minutes

INGREDIENTS

| **1** | 4 swordfish steaks, about 5 oz each |

| **2** | 4–5 small ripe tomatoes |

| **3** | 16 Kalamata olives in brine, drained |

| **4** | 2 tablespoons chopped flat-leaf parsley |

| **5** | 7 oz couscous |

PANTRY

salt and black pepper

Swordfish with Couscous & Salsa

■ Season the swordfish steaks with salt and pepper.

■ Dice or quarter the tomatoes and transfer them to a bowl with all the juices. Remove the pits from the olives and chop the flesh if the pieces are still large. Stir them into the tomatoes with the parsley, season to taste, and set aside.

■ Cook the couscous according to the instructions on the package and set aside.

■ Meanwhile, cook the swordfish steaks, 2 at a time, on a preheated hot ridged grill pan. Cook on the first side for 4 minutes, without disturbing them, then turn and cook for another minute.

■ Serve the swordfish and couscous immediately, topped with the olive and tomato salsa and accompanied with a green salad, if desired.

SERVES 4

Calories per serving 293
Preparation time 10 minutes
Cooking time 20 minutes

INGREDIENTS

1 2 (13 oz) cans cannellini beans, drained and rinsed

2 2 tablespoons chopped parsley, plus sprigs to garnish

3 16 baby leeks

4 16 large scallops, shelled and prepared

PANTRY

2 garlic cloves; 7 fl oz vegetable stock;
2 teaspoons olive oil; 3 tablespoons water

Scallops with White Bean Purée

■ Place the beans, garlic, and stock in a saucepan, bring to a boil and simmer for 10 minutes. Remove from the heat, drain off any excess liquid, then mash with a potato masher and stir in the parsley. Keep warm.

■ Heat half the oil in a nonstick skillet, add the leeks and fry for 2 minutes, then add the measured water. Cover and simmer for 5–6 minutes until tender.

■ Meanwhile, heat the remaining oil in a small skillet, add the scallops and fry for 1 minute on each side. Serve with the white bean purée and leeks.

SERVES 4

Calories per serving 302 (excluding wholegrain rice)
Preparation time 15 minutes
Cooking time about 30 minutes

INGREDIENTS

1	1 red bell pepper, halved and seeded
2	8 dry black olives, pitted
3	2 teaspoons capers
4	8 shallots, peeled
5	4 beef fillet steaks, about 5¼ oz each

PANTRY

2 garlic cloves; 1 tablespoon olive oil; 2 fl oz balsamic vinegar; 1 teaspoon firmly packed light brown sugar; salt and black pepper

Beef Fillet with Red Pepper Crust

■ Cook the pepper under a preheated hot broiler until the skin blackens. Remove and cover with damp paper towel until it is cool enough to handle, then peel and chop.

■ Blend together the garlic, olives, 1 teaspoon of the oil, the capers, and the chopped red pepper.

■ Put the shallots and the remaining oil in a small pan. Cover and cook, stirring frequently, over low heat for 15 minutes. Add the vinegar and sugar and cook uncovered, stirring frequently, for another 5 minutes.

■ Season the steaks and cook, 2 at a time, in a preheated heavy skillet or ridged grill pan. Cook on one side, then transfer to a baking sheet. Top each steak with some red pepper mix. Bake in a preheated oven, at 400°F, for 5 minutes or according to taste.

Let stand in a warm place for 5 minutes before serving with the balsamic shallots and, if desired, steamed wholegrain rice.

TRY IT WITH MUSHROOMS

Blend 11½ oz chopped mushrooms with 2 crushed garlic cloves, 1 chopped onion, 1 tablespoon olive oil and seasoning. Cook as in the main recipe for 10 minutes or until reduced down to concentrate. Add juice of ½ lemon, 2 tablespoons chopped fresh parsley, and a dash of brandy, then cook for another 5 minutes. Cook the steaks as in the main recipe and top with the mushroom mixture. Calories per serving 271

Calories per serving 499
Preparation time 5 minutes
Cooking time 10 minutes

INGREDIENTS

1   **4 salmon fillets, about 7 oz each**

2   **1½ teaspoon cumin seeds, crushed**

3   **1 teaspoon smoked or ordinary paprika**

4   **2 zucchini, sliced into thin ribbons**

PANTRY

3 tablespoons firmly packed light brown sugar;
2 garlic cloves, crushed; 1 tablespoon white wine
vinegar; 3 tablespoons groundnut oil; salt and
black pepper; lemon wedges, to serve

Sugar & Spice Salmon

■ Put the salmon fillets in a lightly oiled
roasting pan. Mix together the sugar, garlic,
1 teaspoon of the cumin seeds, paprika,
vinegar, and a little salt in a bowl, then
spread the mixture all over the fish so that
it is thinly coated. Drizzle with 1 tablespoon
of the oil.

■ Bake in a preheated oven, at 425°F,
for 10 minutes or until the fish is cooked
through.

■ Meanwhile, heat the remaining oil in a
large skillet, add the remaining crushed
cumin seeds and fry for 10 seconds. Add
the zucchini ribbons, season with salt and
pepper, and stir-fry for 2–3 minutes until
just softened.

■ Transfer to warm serving plates and
serve the salmon on top, garnished with
lemon wedges.

SERVES 2

Calories per serving 490
Preparation time 10 minutes
Cooking time 9 minutes

INGREDIENTS

1   3 lb small farmed mussels

2   ¼ pint dry hard cider

3   3½ oz heavy cream

4   2 tablespoons chopped parsley

PANTRY

2 garlic cloves, chopped; 1 onion, diced; salt
and black pepper

Mussels with Hard Cider

■ Wash the mussels thoroughly and put
in a large saucepan with the garlic, diced
onion, and cider. Bring to a boil, cover and
cook over medium heat for 4–5 minutes
until all the shells have opened. Discard any
that remain closed after cooking.

■ Strain the mussels through a colander
and put in a large bowl, cover with foil and
place in a very low oven to keep warm.

■ Pass the cooking juices through a fine
sieve into a clean saucepan and bring to
a boil. Whisk in the cream and simmer for
3–4 minutes, or until thickened slightly.
Season to taste with salt and pepper.

■ Pour the sauce over the mussels,
sprinkle with the parsley and serve
immediately.

ASIAN FLAVORS

Wash the mussels thoroughly and put in a large saucepan with 2 sliced garlic cloves, 2 teaspoons grated fresh ginger, 1 finely diced onion, and 1 sliced red chile. Add a splash of water and cook as in the main recipe. Strain the mussels and keep warm. Strain the cooking juices through a fine sieve into a clean saucepan. Whisk in 3½ oz coconut cream and heat through. Pour over the mussels and served garnished with chopped fresh cilantro. Calories per serving 314

SERVES 4

Calories per serving 411
Preparation time 5 minutes
Cooking time 15-20 minutes

INGREDIENTS

1	**4 boneless, skinless chicken breasts, about 7 oz each**
2	**¼ pint freshly squeezed orange juice, plus 1 small orange, sliced**
3	**2 tablespoons chopped mint**
4	**1 tablespoon butter**
5	**7 oz couscous**

PANTRY

3 tablespoons olive oil; salt and black pepper

Chicken with Orange & Mint

■ Season the chicken breasts to taste with salt and pepper. Heat the oil in a large nonstick skillet, add the chicken breasts and cook over medium heat, turning once, for 4-5 minutes or until golden all over.

■ Pour in the orange juice, add the orange slices, and bring to a gentle simmer. Cover tightly, reduce the heat to low and cook gently for 8-10 minutes or until the chicken is cooked through. Add the chopped mint and butter and stir together to mix well. Cook over high heat, stirring, for 2 minutes. Serve immediately with couscous.

SERVES 4

Calories per serving 302
Preparation time 10 minutes
Cooking time 6–8 minutes

INGREDIENTS

1 12 sardines, cleaned and gutted

2 2 tablespoons harissa

3 chopped cilantro, to garnish

PANTRY

2 tablespoons olive oil; juice of 1 lemon, plus lemon
wedges, to serve; salt flakes and black pepper

Moroccan Grilled Sardines

■ Heat the broiler on the hottest setting.
Rinse the sardines and pat dry with paper
towel. Make several deep slashes on both
sides of each fish with a sharp knife.

■ Mix the harissa with the oil and lemon
juice to make a thin paste. Rub into the
sardines on both sides. Put the sardines
on a lightly oiled baking sheet. Cook under
the broiler for 3–4 minutes on each side,
depending on their size, or until cooked
through. Season to taste with salt flakes and
pepper and serve immediately garnished
with cilantro and with lemon wedges.

BAKE WITH PESTO

Line a medium ovenproof dish with 2 sliced tomatoes and 2 sliced onions. Prepare the sardines as in the main recipe, then rub ¼ cup pesto over the fish instead of the harissa paste and arrange in a single layer on top of the tomatoes and onions. Cover with foil and bake in a preheated oven, at 400°F, for 20–25 minutes or until the fish is cooked through. Calories per serving 375

Calories per serving 148
Preparation time 20 minutes
Cooking time 4–7 minutes

INGREDIENTS

1   2 thick-cut sirloin steaks, about 1 lb in total

2   7 oz natural yogurt

3   1–1½ teaspoons horseradish sauce (to taste)

4   5 oz mixed green leaves

5   3½ oz button mushrooms, sliced

PANTRY

3 teaspoons colored peppercorns, coarsely crushed; coarse salt flakes; 1 garlic clove, crushed; 1 red onion, thinly sliced; 1 tablespoon olive oil salt and black pepper

Peppered Beef with Salad

- Trim the fat from the steaks and rub the meat with the crushed peppercorns and salt flakes.

- Mix together the yogurt, horseradish sauce, and garlic and season to taste with salt and pepper. Add the greens, mushrooms, and most of the red onion and toss together gently.

- Heat the oil in a skillet, add the steaks and cook over high heat for 2 minutes until browned. Turn over and cook for 2 minutes for medium rare, 3–4 minutes for medium, or 5 minutes for well done.

- Spoon the salad into the center of six serving plates. Thinly slice the steaks and arrange the pieces on top, then garnish with the remaining red onion.

SERVES 4

Calories per serving 475
Preparation time 12 minutes, plus marinating
Cooking time 8 minutes

INGREDIENTS

1	**1 egg, lightly beaten**
2	**1 lb boneless, skinless chicken breasts, cut into ¼ inch slices**
3	**1 scallion, diagonally sliced into ¾ inch lengths**
4	**5½ oz long-grain rice**

PANTRY

2 garlic cloves, sliced; 2 small pieces of lemon peel, plus juice of 1 lemon; 2 tablespoons cornflour; 1 tablespoon rapeseed or olive oil; lemon slices, to garnish

Low-fat Lemon Chicken

■ Mix the egg, garlic, and lemon peel together in a shallow dish, add the chicken and let marinate for 10–15 minutes.

■ Remove the lemon peel and add the cornflour to the marinated chicken. Mix thoroughly to distribute the cornflour evenly among the chicken slices.

■ Heat the oil in a wok over high heat until the oil starts to shimmer. Add the chicken slices, making sure you leave a little space between them, and fry for 2 minutes on each side.

■ Reduce the heat to medium and stir-fry for 1 more minute or until the chicken is browned and cooked. Turn up the heat and pour in the lemon juice. Add the scallion, garnish with lemon slices, and serve immediately with boiled rice.

SERVES 4

Calories per serving 308 (excluding pasta)
Preparation time 10 minutes
Cooking time 10 minutes

INGREDIENTS

1	**4 lamb leg steaks, about 4 oz each, fat trimmed off**
2	**6 tablespoons chopped flat-leaf parsley, plus extra whole sprigs to garnish**
3	**12 sundried tomatoes**
4	**2 tablespoons caperberries, rinsed**

PANTRY

1 garlic clove, crushed; 1 tablespoon lemon juice;
1 tablespoon olive oil; salt and black pepper

Grilled Lamb with Caperberries

■ Season the meat and cook under a preheated hot broiler for about 5 minutes on each side until golden.

■ Reserve ¼ cup of the chopped parsley. Blend the remaining parsley with the garlic, tomatoes, lemon juice, and oil.

■ Spoon the tomato sauce over the lamb. Sprinkle over the reserved chopped flat-leaf parsley and add the caperberries. Garnish with whole parsley sprigs and serve with pasta, if desired.

TRY A TAPENADE

Use black olive tapenade instead of the dressing and stir all the parsley through it. To make your own tapenade, blend 5 oz pitted black olives, 3 tablespoons extra virgin olive oil, 1 garlic clove, and 2 salted anchovies in a food processor with black pepper and add chopped flat-leaf parsley to taste. Calories per serving (with steak) 357

SERVES 2

Calories per serving 452
Preparation time 15 minutes
Cooking time 5 minutes

INGREDIENTS

1 10–12 prepared baby squid, about 12 oz including tentacles, cleaned

2 2 red chiles, seeded and finely chopped

3 1 inch piece of fresh ginger, peeled and grated

4 3½ oz freshly grated coconut

5 mixed greens, to serve

STORECUPBOARD

4 lemons, halved, plus finely grated zest and juice of 2 lemons; ¼ cup groundnut oil; 1–2 tablespoons chilli oil; 1 tablespoon white wine vinegar

Coconut Citrus Squid

■ Cut down the side of each squid and lay flat on a cutting board. Using a sharp knife, lightly crisscross the inside flesh.

■ Mix the lemon juice, chiles, ginger, coconut, oils, and vinegar together. Toss the squid in half the dressing until coated.

■ Heat a ridged grill pan until smoking hot, add the lemons, cut side down, and cook for 2 minutes until well charred. Remove from the pan and set aside. Keeping the grill pan very hot, add the squid pieces and cook for 1 minute. Turn them over and cook for another minute or until they turn white, lose their transparency, and are charred.

■ Transfer the squid to a cutting board and cut into strips. Drizzle with the remaining dressing and serve immediately with the charred lemons and mixed greens.

SOMETHING SWEET

SERVES 12

Calories per serving 282
Preparation time 1 minute
Cooking time 4 minutes

INGREDIENTS

1   **4 oz popcorn kernels**

2   **2¼ sticks butter**

3   **2 tablespoons cocoa powder**

PANTRY

1¼ cups firmly packed light brown sugar

Caramel & Chocolate Popcorn

■ Microwave the popcorn kernels in a large bowl with a lid on high (900 watts) for 4 minutes. Alternatively, cook in a pan with a lid on the stove, on medium heat, for a few minutes until popping.

■ Meanwhile, gently heat the butter, sugar, and cocoa powder in a pan until the sugar has dissolved and the butter has melted.

■ Stir the warm popcorn into the mixture and serve.

MAKE IT CHEWY

Omit the sugar and cocoa. Microwave the popcorn as in the main recipe, then gently heat 5 oz chewy caramels, 1⅛ stick butter, 4 oz marshmallows and 2 oz dark chocolate in a pan until melted. Serve as in the main recipe. Calories per serving 341

SERVES 4

Calories per serving 177
Preparation time 5 minutes

INGREDIENTS

1   **10 oz raspberries, coarsely chopped**

2   **4 shortbread fingers, crushed**

3   **13 oz low-fat fromage frais**

PANTRY

2 tablespoons confectioners' sugar or artificial
sweetener

Raspberry Shortbread Cups

■ Reserving a few raspberries for
decoration, combine all the ingredients
in a bowl. Spoon into 4 serving dishes.

■ Serve immediately, decorated with
the reserved raspberries.

MAKE AN ETON MESS

Use 4 meringue nests and 10 oz strawberries. Hull and halve or quarter the strawberries, then add them to the fromage frais with the sugar or sweetener. Break the meringues into chunks and fold them through the fromage frais, then pile into glasses and serve. Calories per serving 143

SERVES 2

Calories per serving 131
Preparation time 10 minutes, plus chilling
Cooking time 1–2 minutes

INGREDIENTS

1	½ small mango, peeled, pitted, and thinly sliced
2	1 passion fruit, halved and flesh scooped out
3	5 oz low-fat natural yogurt
4	3½ oz sour cream
5	a few drops of vanilla extract

PANTRY

½ tablespoon confectioners' sugar; 1 tablespoon Demerara sugar

Mango & Passion Fruit Brûlées

■ Divide the mango slices evenly between 2 ramekins.

■ Mix together the passion fruit flesh, yogurt, sour cream, confectioners' sugar, and vanilla extract in a bowl, then spoon the mixture over the mango. Tap each ramekin to level the surface.

■ Sprinkle on the Demerara sugar, then cook the brûlées under a hot broiler for 1–2 minutes until the sugar has melted. Chill for about 30 minutes before serving.

SERVES 4

Calories per serving 112 (excluding cookies)
Preparation time 5 minutes, plus standing

INGREDIENTS

| 1 | 2 ripe bananas |

| 2 | ½ oz crystallized or candied ginger, finely chopped, plus extra to decorate |

| 3 | 5 oz low-fat natural yogurt |

PANTRY

juice of ½ lemon; 8 teaspoons firmly packed dark brown sugar

Banana & Brown Sugar Ripples

■ Toss the bananas in a little lemon juice and mash on a plate with a fork. Add the ginger and yogurt and mix together. Spoon one-third of the mixture into the bases of 4 small dessert glasses.

■ Sprinkle 1 teaspoon of the sugar over each dessert. Spoon half of the remaining banana mixture on top, then repeat with a second layer of sugar. Complete the layers with the remaining banana mixture and decorate with a little extra ginger, cut into slightly larger pieces.

■ Let the puddings stand for 10–15 minutes for the sugar to dissolve and form a syrupy layer between the layers of banana yogurt. Serve with dainty cookies, if desired.

Calories per serving 204
Preparation time 10 minutes
Cooking time 30 minutes

INGREDIENTS

1	4 oz reduced-fat sunflower spread
2	2 eggs
3	2 oz cocoa, sieved, plus extra to decorate
4	2 oz dark chocolate, chopped
5	1 teaspoon chocolate extract

PANTRY

⅔ cup soft light brown sugar; ½ cup plus 1 tablespoon all-purpose flour; ½ teaspoon baking powder; salt

Chocolate Brownies

■ Grease and line a 7 inch square deep cake pan.

■ Beat together the sunflower spread, eggs, and sugar. Stir in the flour, and cocoa, then add the chocolate and chocolate extract. Stir in 1 teaspoon boiling water and a pinch of salt.

■ Transfer the mixture to the prepared pan and bake in a preheated oven, at 375°F, for 30 minutes or until a toothpick comes out clean when inserted in the center. Let cool in the pan then cut into 9 squares. Dust with a little cocoa powder to serve.

MAKES 24 SQUARES

Calories per serving 201
Preparation time 25 minutes, plus cooling
Cooking time 55 minutes

INGREDIENTS

1	**1¾ sticks lightly salted butter, softened, plus extra for greasing**
2	**7½ oz stoned dates, chopped**
3	**¼ pint heavy cream**
4	**2 teaspoons vanilla bean paste**
5	**3 eggs**

PANTRY

¼ pint water; generous ¾ cup firmly packed light brown sugar; ½ cup superfine sugar; 1⅓ cup all-purpose flour; ½ teaspoon baking powder

Caramel & Date Squares

■ Grease and line an 11 × 7 inch shallow baking pan with nonstick parchment paper. Put 4 oz of the dates in a saucepan with the water and bring to a boil. Reduce the heat and cook gently for 5 minutes or until the dates are pulpy. Place in a bowl and let cool. Put the cream, light brown sugar, and 5 tablespoons of the butter in a small saucepan and heat gently until the sugar dissolves. Bring to a boil and boil for 5 minutes or until thickened and caramelized. Let cool.

■ Put the remaining butter in a bowl with the superfine sugar, vanilla bean paste, and eggs, sift in the flour and baking powder and beat with a handheld electric whisk until pale and creamy. Beat in the cooked dates and 3½ fl oz of the caramel mixture. Transfer to the pan and level the surface. Sprinkle with the remaining dates.

■ Bake in a preheated oven, 350°F, for 25 minutes, or until just firm. Spoon the remaining caramel on top and return to the oven for 15 minutes until the caramel has firmed. Transfer to a wire rack to cool.

MAKES 12

Calories per serving 240
Preparation time 10 minutes, plus chilling
Cooking time 3 minutes

INGREDIENTS

1 7 oz milk chocolate, broken into pieces

2 2 tablespoons corn syrup

3 2 oz olive oil spread, plus extra for greasing

4 4 oz cornflakes

Chocolate Cornflake Bars

- Melt the chocolate with the syrup and olive oil spread in a bowl over a pan of simmering water.

- Stir in the cornflakes and mix everything together.

- Grease a 11 × 7 inch pan. Transger the mixture into the pan, chill until set, then cut into 12 bars.

Calories per serving 345
Preparation time 25 minutes, plus proving
Cooking time 12–15 minutes

INGREDIENTS

1   **1 tablespoon fast-acting dried yeast**

2   **¼ stick slightly salted butter, melted**

3   **½ pint hot milk, plus extra if required**

4   **2 teaspoons vanilla extract**

5   **pink food coloring**

PANTRY

3¾ cups white bread flour; ¼ cup superfine sugar;
1½ cups fondant sugar

Simple Iced Buns

■ Mix together the flour, superfine sugar, and yeast in a bowl. Add the butter, milk, and vanilla and mix to a fairly soft dough, adding a dash more milk or hot water if the dough feels dry. Knead the dough for 10 minutes on a floured surface until smooth and elastic. Put in a lightly oiled bowl, cover with plastic wrap and let rise in a warm place for about 1 hour or until doubled in size.

■ Punch the dough to deflate it, then divide into 10 even-sized pieces on a floured surface and shape each into a sausage shape. Place, well spaced apart, on a large greased baking sheet. Cover loosely with greased plastic wrap and let rise for 30 minutes.

■ Bake in a preheated oven, at 400°F, for 12–15 minutes until risen and pale golden (placing a roasting pan filled with ¾ inch hot water on the lower shelf to prevent a firm crust forming). Transfer to a wire rack to cool.

■ Make the icing. Sift the fondant sugar into a bowl and gradually beat in a little water, a teaspoonful at a time, to make a smooth, spreadable icing. Spread half over 5 of the buns. Add a dash of pink food coloring to the remaining icing and spread over the rest of the buns. Best eaten freshly baked.

MAKES ABOUT 30

Calories per serving 80
Preparation time 20 minutes, plus setting
Cooking time 30 minutes

INGREDIENTS

| 1 | 1⅛ stick lightly salted butter, melted, plus extra for greasing |

| 2 | 2 teaspoons cardamom pods |

| 3 | 3 eggs |

PANTRY

1 cup all-purpose flour, plus extra for dusting; ⅔ cup superfine sugar; finely grated zest of 1 lemon, plus 2 tablespoons lemon juice; ½ teaspoon baking powder; ⅓ cup confectioners' sugar, sifted, plus extra for dusting

Lemon Glazed Cardamom Madeleines

■ Grease a madeleine tray with melted butter and dust with flour. Tap out the excess flour.

■ Crush the cardamom pods using a pestle and mortar to release the seeds. Remove the shells and crush the seeds a little further.

■ Put the eggs, superfine sugar, lemon zest and crushed cardamom seeds in a heatproof bowl and rest the bowl over a saucepan of gently simmering water. Whisk with a handheld electric whisk until the mixture is thick and pale and the mixture leaves a trail when lifted.

■ Sift the flour and baking powder into the bowl and gently fold in using a large metal spoon. Drizzle the melted butter around the edges of the mixture and fold the ingredients together to combine. Spoon the mixture into the madeleine sections until about two-thirds full. (Keep the remaining mixture for a second batch.)

■ Bake in a preheated oven, at 425°F, for about 10 minutes until risen and golden. Leave in the tray for 5 minutes, then transfer to a wire rack.

■ Make the glaze by putting the lemon juice in a bowl and beating in the confectioners' sugar. Brush over the madeleines and let set. Make a second batch with the remaining batter. Serve lightly dusted with confectioners' sugar.

Calories per serving 168 (excluding cookies)
Preparation time 10 minutes

INGREDIENTS

1 | 1 large mango, peeled, pitted and cut into chunks

2 | 1½ lb fat-free natural yogurt

3 | 1–2 tablespoons agave nectar, to taste

4 | 1 vanilla pod, split in half lengthwise

5 | 4 passion fruit, halved

Creamy Mango & Passion Fruit

■ Place the mango in a food processor or blender and blend to a purée.

■ Put the yogurt and agave nectar in a large bowl, scrape in the seeds from the vanilla pod and beat together. Gently fold in the mango purée and spoon into tall glasses or glass serving dishes.

■ Scoop the seeds from the passion fruit and spoon over the mango yogurt. Serve immediately with thin cookies, if desired.

TRY BLACKCURRANTS

Purée 8 oz blackcurrants as in the main recipe and fold into the yogurt with the agave nectar, according to taste, and 1 teaspoon almond essence. Spoon into tall, glass serving dishes and sprinkle with toasted almonds, to serve. Calories per serving 143

MAKES 16

Calories per serving 217
Preparation time 30 minutes
Cooking time 45–60 minutes

INGREDIENTS

| 1 | 3 egg whites |

| 2 | 2 oz shelled pistachio nuts, finely chopped |

| 3 | 5 oz dark chocolate, broken into pieces |

| 4 | ¼ pint heavy cream |

PANTRY

generous ¾ cup superfine sugar

Pistachio & Chocolate Meringues

■ Whisk the egg whites in a large clean bowl until stiff. Gradually whisk in the sugar, a teaspoonful at a time, until it has all been added. Whisk for a few minutes more until the meringue mixture is thick and glossy.

■ Fold in the pistachios then spoon heaped teaspoonfuls of the mixture into rough swirly mounds on 2 large baking sheets lined with nonstick parchment paper.

■ Bake in a preheated oven, at 225°F, for 45–60 minutes or until the meringues are firm and may be easily peeled off the paper. Let cool still on the paper.

■ Melt the chocolate in a heatproof bowl set over a saucepan of gently simmering water. Lift the meringues off the paper and dip their bases into the chocolate to coat. Return to the paper, tilted on their sides

and leave in a cool place until the chocolate has hardened.

■ To serve, whip the cream until it just holds its shape, then use it to sandwich the meringues together in pairs. Arrange the pairs in paper cake cases, if desired, on a cake plate or stand. Eat on the day they are filled. (Left plain, the meringues will keep for 2–3 days.)

MAKES 20 SQUARES

Calories per serving 248
Preparation time 30 minutes
Cooking time 30–35 minutes

INGREDIENTS

1	1 large mango
2	4 tablespoons apricot jam
3	2 kiwifruit, sliced
4	2¼ sticks soft margarine
5	4 eggs

PANTRY

grated zest and juice of 2 lemons; ⅔ cup superfine sugar; ⅔ cup firmly packed light brown sugar; 2 cups all-purpose flour; 2 teaspoons baking powder

Mango & Kiwi Upside Down Cake

■ Cut a thick slice off each side of the mango to reveal the large flat central pit. Cut the flesh away from the pit then peel and slice.

■ Mix the apricot jam with the juice of 1 of the lemons then spoon into the base of a 7 × 11 inch roasting pan lined with nonstick parchment paper. Arrange the mango and kiwi fruit randomly over the top.

■ Put the lemon zest and rest of the juice in a mixing bowl or a food processor, add the remaining ingredients and beat until smooth. Spoon over the top of the fruit and spread the surface level. Bake in a preheated oven, at 350°F, for 30–35 minutes until well risen, the cake is golden, and it springs back when gently pressed with a fingertip.

■ Let cool in the pan for 10 minutes then invert the pan onto a wire rack, remove the pan and lining paper and let cool completely. Cut into 20 pieces and serve warm. This is best eaten on the day it is made.

MAKES 14 SQUARES

Calories per serving 102
Preparation time 10 minutes, plus setting
Cooking time 5 minutes

INGREDIENTS

1	7 oz marshmallows, halved
2	3 tablespoons unsalted butter, diced
3	3½ oz crisped rice cereal
4	sprinkles, to decorate

Marshmallow Crackle Squares

■ Reserve 2 oz of the marshmallows. Put 2 tablespoons of the butter and the remaining marshmallows into a saucepan and heat very gently until melted. Remove from the heat and stir in the cereal until evenly coated.

■ Spoon the mixture into an 7 inch square shallow baking pan, greased and lined with parchment paper, and pack down firmly with the back of a lightly oiled spoon.

■ Place the remaining butter and reserved marshmallows in a small saucepan and heat gently until melted. Drizzle into the pan in lines, then sprinkle the sprinkles over the top. Leave in a cool place for 2 hours or until firm.

■ Turn the set mixture out of the pan onto a board, peel off the lining paper and cut into small squares.

SERVES 4

Calories per serving 220
Preparation time 5 minutes
Cooking time 8–10 minutes

INGREDIENTS

1   **4 bananas, unpeeled**

2   **½ cup fat-free Greek yogurt**

3   **¼ cup oatmeal or fine oats**

4   **4 oz blueberries**

5   **honey, to serve**

Grilled Bananas with Blueberries

■ Heat a ridged grill pan over medium-hot heat, add the bananas and grill for 8–10 minutes, or until the skins are beginning to blacken, turning occasionally.

■ Transfer the bananas to serving dishes and, using a sharp knife, cut open lengthwise. Spoon over the yogurt and sprinkle with the oatmeal or oats and blueberries. Serve immediately, drizzled with a little honey.

A DELICIOUS YOGURT

Mix ½ teaspoon ground ginger with the yogurt in a bowl. Sprinkle with 2–4 tablespoons soft dark brown sugar, according to taste, the oatmeal and ¼ cup golden raisins. Let stand for 5 minutes before serving. Calories per serving 208

MAKES 10 SLICES

Calories per serving 373
Preparation time 20 minutes, plus cooling
Cooking time 1 hour 25 minutes

INGREDIENTS

| 1 | 8 oz stoned dates, coarsely chopped |

| 2 | 2 small very ripe bananas |

| 3 | 1⅜ sticks slightly salted butter, softened |

| 4 | 2 eggs |

| 5 | 3½ fl oz milk |

PANTRY

finely grated zest and juice of 1 lemon; 3½ fl oz water; ¾ cup superfine sugar; 2¼ cups all-purpose flour; 2 teaspoons baking powder

Date & Banana Ripple Slice

■ Put 7 oz of the dates in a small saucepan with the lemon zest and juice and measured water. Bring to a boil, then reduce the heat and simmer gently for 5 minutes until the dates are soft and pulpy. Mash the mixture with a fork until fairly smooth. Let cool.

■ Mash the bananas to a purée in a bowl, then add the butter, sugar, eggs, milk, flour and baking powder and beat together until the mixture is smooth.

■ Spoon a third of the mixture into a greased and lined 2½ lb or 2½ pint loaf pan and level the surface. Spoon over half the date purée and spread evenly. Add half the remaining cake mixture and spread with the remaining purée. Add the remaining cake mixture and level the surface.

■ Sprinkle with the reserved dates and bake in a preheated oven, at 325°F, for about 1 hour 20 minutes or until risen and a toothpick inserted into the center comes out clean. Cool in the pan for 15 minutes, then loosen around the sides and transfer to a wire rack. Peel off the lining paper and let cake cool completely.

SERVES 6

Calories per serving 216
Preparation time 30 minutes, plus freezing
Cooking time 2–4 minutes

INGREDIENTS

1 1 (14 oz) can pitted lychees in light syrup

2 1 (14 fl oz) can full-fat coconut milk

3 grated zest and juice of 1 lime, plus extra pared lime peel, to decorate (optional)

4 3 kiwi fruit, peeled and cut into wedges, to decorate

PANTRY

¼ cup superfine sugar

Lychee & Coconut Sherbet

■ Drain the syrup from the can of lychees into a saucepan, add the sugar and heat gently until the sugar has dissolved. Boil for 2 minutes, then take off the heat and let cool.

■ Purée the lychees in a food processor or liquidizer until smooth, or rub through a sieve. Mix with the coconut milk, lime zest and juice. Stir in the sugar syrup when it is cool.

■ Pour into a shallow plastic container and freeze for 4 hours or until mushy. Beat with a fork or blend in a food processor or liquidizer until smooth. Pour back into the plastic container and freeze for 4 hours or overnight until solid. (Alternatively, freeze in an electric ice-cream machine for 20 minutes, then transfer to a plastic box and freeze until required.)

■ Allow to soften for 15 minutes at room temperature before serving, then scoop into dishes (or chocolate cups if preferred, see right) and decorate with kiwi fruit wedges and pared lime zest curls, if desired.

SERVE IN CHOCOLATE CUPS

For chocolate cups, to serve the sherbet in, melt 5 oz dark chocolate over a pan of simmering water, then divide between 4 squares of nonstick parchment paper and spread into rough-shaped circles about 6 inches in diameter. Drape the paper over upturned glass tumblers, with the chocolate uppermost, so that the paper falls in soft folds. Chill until set, then lift the paper and chocolate off the tumblers, turn over and carefully ease the paper away. Calories per serving 195

SERVES 6

Calories per serving 327
Preparation time 1 minute
Cooking time 4 minutes

INGREDIENTS

1	10 oz plain dark chocolate
2	1 lb fat-free fromage frais
3	1 teaspoon vanilla extract

Warm Chocolate Pudding

■ Melt the chocolate in a heatproof bowl set over a pan of simmering water, then remove from the heat.

■ Add the fromage frais and vanilla extract and quickly stir together.

■ Divide the chocolate pudding among 6 little pots or glasses and serve immediately.

MAKE IT CAPPUCCINO

Melt the dark chocolate with 2 tablespoons very strong espresso coffee. Divide among 6 espresso cups, finishing each with 1 teaspoon regular fromage frais and a dusting of cocoa powder. Calories per serving 339

INDEX

PICTURE CREDITS